Critical Thinking

50 Best Strategies to Think Smart and Clear,
Get Logical Thinking, and Improve
Your Decision Making Skills

Christ Lewis

ISBN-10: 1505898641
ISBN-13: 978-1505898644

DEDICATION

This book is dedicated to people of all genders and ages who wish to know all about how to think smart and clear, get logical thinking, and improve your decision making skills with many strategies. Practicing following each strategy will make your thinking more effective and efficient.

CONTENTS

Critical Thinking

Introduction

"Whatever the mind can conceive and believe, it can achieve." This might be an overused quotation to many of us; still, it is the secret to all that has been and all that will ever be. Yes, critical thinking is the secret. The human mind is so powerful and it is factual that everything that's happening in our life is attracted by our thoughts. Thoughts become things.

Many of us haven't reached our full potential. We can be someone. But oftentimes, we think that we cannot. This is the main reason which hinders our success. That thought is a big lie. We are highly capable and we were designed to have the capability to shape our destiny. However, the superb potential that lies within remains dormant and untapped. It is mostly undeveloped. That is why we need to train and improve our thinking. Humans have the unique gift to be able to learn anything they want. The best way to improve our thinking is to train. It is the same training to improve in sports, dancing, or playing musical instruments, only with a different method. It requires patience and hard work. Such improvement will only take place with willingness, commitment, and dedication to learn. On the other hand, we will reap painful consequences if we do not take this seriously.

This development we desire is a process that requires a lot of work. No matter the will, it is impossible to become a critical thinker overnight. It is a challenging, long-term process. It might even take a couple of years just to change our thinking habits. The ideal and vital characteristics of a true critical thinker require an even longer period to attain full development.

How can we train our minds? How can critical thinking be attained? How can we apply critical thinking on a daily basis? How can we fuel our minds and reach our full potential to live the life we desire?

This ebook explains 50 strategies that anyone with the burning desire to learn and improve can use. As the strategies are explained and described, certain tips and drills will be given as your assignment.

However, this book only provides the content; the work is up to you. You decide whether you embrace the challenge or not. Remember, there are only two types of pain: the pain of commitment and the pain of regret.

Accept

Yes, we need to accept that problems lie in our thinking. It is a need to say yes to the challenge in improving our thinking. Most people who begin the challenge are unaware of significant problems in our thinking. They are the unreflective thinkers. Hence, we need to get out of this stage. Sometimes our ego and pride hinder us from committing to learning; we likewise need to get rid of these to begin regular practice. So, ask yourself over and over again, do you fully accept that you were once an unreflective thinker? If you consistently answer yes, then you are ready.

Start accepting yourself with the following tips:

Above all, accept yourself without hatred.

Use non-blaming and simple phrases. In your case, say "I am an unreflective thinker".

Assess yourself without blaming and self-hate. Blaming only leads to being defensive, which will bring out your ego and pride.

Perform relaxation breathing if you begin feeling defensive and self-hating.

Affirmative statements as you embark towards change will always help.

A good laugh will make acceptance of your weakness, which is unreflective thinking, easier.

Remember that improving critical thinking is a part of your personal growth. You must accept yourself and your weakness to give way to a better you.

Evaluate your thinking

Evaluate your weaknesses and strengths in thinking. The following are questions you might ask yourself.

What was on my mind today? Did negative thoughts disturb me today?

Did I figure anything out today?

When did I do my best thinking today?

When did I do my worst?

Have I done something beneficial to my goals today?

If I had a chance to repeat the day, what would I do differently? Why?

If every day was lived in this manner for a year, will something be accomplished at the end of the year?

Now, evaluate yourself. Of course, it is necessary to ponder and reflect upon the questions. You are now a challenged thinker, aware of your problems in thinking. Your pattern of thinking will be noticeable in the soonest time.

Make the most of your time

We all waste some time. Applying time management tactics seems to be hard work for all of us. We do not use the whole of our time in a productive manner. We even skip one activity to prioritize another in some instances. We realize later on that none of them was enjoyed. We even get easily frustrated and irritated with small matters or matters we could never control. We do not plan well, and our poor planning yields us regrets and consequences. We end up with problems that could have been heeded, solved, and avoided. Here is an example. If we left earlier to get to our destination, the long hours we suffer in a traffic jam could have been avoided. We even waste time over thinking of our regrets in the past. Or we just blankly stare off into space sometimes.

Time is irreversible. It is gone. We should have spent it well and carefully examined our options. In that way, we would never have wasted any of it. So next time, why not take advantage of the time you normally waste by improving your critical thinking?

Maximize your time for critical thinking through the following:

1. Read an interesting book or feature when you're feeling idle.
2. Write down your thoughts about different topics.
3. Test your brain regularly through quizzes or puzzles.
4. Practice freethinking or logic-based thinking as you read.

Avoid being idle by maximizing your time spent for improving critical thinking. Challenge and train your thinking whenever you have a spare time and start building your foundation towards being a critical thinker.

Character transformation

You need to reshape your character. Now you will need to choose one intellectual trait that you will strive to improve each month. It may be intellectual perseverance, courage, humility, empathy, or autonomy. Once you have done so, perform the following steps:

Concentrate on how to improve your chosen trait. For example, you may have chosen intellectual humility.

Be aware that denying your mistakes is in fact wrong.

Be aware that ego and arrogance keep one away from educating himself. Own up to your arrogance so you can deal with it. Never think you possess all the knowledge in this world, or thinking that you are as knowledgeable as others.

This is a very crucial step in critical thinking improvement. Character is very important.

Be aware of your emotions

Emotions are a gift to us, and critical thinking strongly depends on our emotional awareness and how we deal with it. We should always systematically and automatically ask ourselves what is our thinking that led to this certain emotion.

For example, when you are feeling sad, ask yourself, "What is the thinking that is making me sad?"

Then, think of other ways you could think about the situation. You can perhaps see humor in the situation. If you can do this effectively, concentrate on the positive thinking, and your emotions will shift along with your thinking.

Analyze your groups

Group influences bear a paramount impact on your thinking and behavior. Most of us live too much in bowing in to pressure brought by the group to which we belong. Every group has a certain set of demeanors and beliefs. Closely analyze what belief you are bowing to and think whether or not you should reject that pressure. It would be best to be with a circle of friends whose ideals you find are agreeable for you.

Analyze your group through the following steps:

1. Take note of the usual topics in the group. Remember that big minds discuss ideas, not gossips. See if your groupmates only blabber gossips or bash others without being factual in their claims.

2. Try starting a discussion about a general topic. Avoid taboo topics at this point, though, because you don't know the group's reaction as of the moment. See if they are willing to share their insights about the topic.

3. Analyze their reactions to your opinions. Opinions are different, but open-mindedness will help in promoting critical thinking and healthy discussions. At this point, you'll gauge the open-minded individuals and those that are one with you in thinking.

Jokes and chats are not bad, especially if it's bonding type with your friends. However, you must spend a lot of time hanging out with open-minded people who encourage healthy discussions about crucial topics to enhance critical thinking.

Change your perception of things

In every situation, we are the ones who give meaning to it. Your current status can be transformed by the way you see it. You have the power in your mind to make your life more fulfilling. A problem is only a problem when you see it as a problem. You can give it either negative or positive definitions. We are sad when we could be happy. We are frustrated when we could be fulfilled. Changing our perception of things will redefine negative thoughts into positive ones, problems as blessings, and regrets and mistakes into chances for growth. The drill is to set a specific guideline for us.

1. Think of recurrent negative situations, which make you feel bad and list them down.

2. Write beside it an alternative response that would bring new perceptions. For example, on your list it says a person of the opposite sex is not attracted to you. This will yield lack of confidence or you may even start to think of your defects. So write down beside it its alternative response. You might say, the person is not yet attracted to me because we just met, not because I am the way I am.

Deal with a problem

During your free time, pick one problem to deal with.

1. Find the problem's logic and identify its elements.

2. Know the problem, and analyze how it relates to your needs, purposes, and goals. State your chosen problem clearly.

3. Determine your options. What will be your action in the short term? What will be your action in the long term? Also, those predicaments beyond your control must be set aside.

4. Know your limitations concerning time, power, and money.

5. Act and apply your chosen options. Also, be ready to change your tactic and analysis as implications of your actions begin to emerge.

Develop your intellectual standards

Universal intellectual standards refer to precision, clarity, relevance, accuracy, depth, breadth, significance, and logicalness. Develop a heightened awareness with one of them each week.

Improve your intellectual standards include a lot of questioning. It's like questioning the importance and details of the things you're reading or hearing. Common questions to ask are the following:

1. Is the point logical or does it make sense?

2. Is it possible to express the same thought using a different angle?

3. Can you elaborate your point?

4. Is the point factual?

5. Can you discuss it in detail?

6. How can you tackle the complex or underlying issues in a point?

7. Is a point relevant to another issue?

Your intellectual standards shouldn't be limited in the superficial knowledge of statistics, depth of used words, and complex statement. Being critical is dissecting these points and questioning their essence in a deeper way.

Get rid of egocentric thinking

Egocentric thinking is having an automatic subconscious bias in favor of oneself. It is evident in human nature yet it is a detrimental form of thinking. Once you start to automatically determine egocentric thinking, you develop along the way an automatic system of self-reflection. Self-reflection is the key to getting rid of egocentric thinking.

Use self-reflection to get rid of egocentrism through these steps:

1. Recognize that you're egocentric. Accept that this is your way of thinking to give way to improving yourself. Thinking about it may be difficult, but recognition and acceptance are the first steps in overcoming egocentrism.

2. Egocentrism is something you can get rid of. This thinking is something that you acquired, which means you can still turn it around. However, remind yourself that getting rid of it may take some time. Be confident in the fact that you'll get there.

3. Stay motivated by thinking about the new and better you. As mentioned earlier, being a critical thinker is a sign of personal growth. The process of changing your thinking may be difficult, but always keep the future in mind for motivation.

Write an intellectual journal

Having an intellectual journal will help you keep track of your progress in improving your critical thinking. Self-assessment would be an easier task through reading your thoughts on a piece of paper. You can have journal entries on a daily or weekly basis.

1. Have a category for each of these four: situation, response, analysis, and assessment.

2. In the situation category, write down a situation that you care about. Describe why it affected your emotions. Focus on one at a time.

3. Write down your response. Be specific and exact in describing how you responded.

4. Analyze what you have written and determine what was exactly happening. Write it down.

5. Lastly, evaluate implications of the analysis. Did you learn anything from the situation? If given a chance, what could you have done differently towards the situation?

Ask questions

Questioning what is heard, read, or seen is one way of developing critical thinking. It was observed that when a toddler appears to be curious, he/she possesses a higher level of intelligence. And the benefits of curiosity don't only apply to toddlers; it also applies to us adults seeking improvement in our patterns of thinking.

It is different from being opinionated in an irrational matter. Having rational questions within us exercises our thinking. Agreeing to certain situations isn't wrong, but always agreeing is a big no. The next time you come across situations, search for self-kept questions. If you are able to answer it all by yourself, then it is a good thing. If not, ask, or search for the answer until you find it. After all, what is a question without an answer?

Ask questions and find answers through the following steps:

1. Use the questions mentioned in the "Develop your intellectual standards" section.

2. Dissect through the point. Get into the thought behind the point by digging deeper into the concept. Look at it in context and compare it with other points presented. See if the concept is logical, factual, interesting, and relevant.

3. Let answers come to you. You will start to unravel answers as you dissect through the point.

4. Search for additional insights. If you're still confused, look for additional insights by searching online or in other related documents.

Remember that asking question is fundamental in critical thinking. Don't be afraid to ask questions and find the answers through researching.

Value and respect other's ideas

Critical thinking is not always about thinking about your personal interest and will for that is a different thing called ego. A true and developed thinker values and respects the ideas of others sincerely. It is a form of humility and another aspect of critical thinking.

1.   Learn to listen because the ideas you were looking for might just be picked up from the person you are talking to.

2.   Do not prejudge. A person might be dressed in rags but still keep in his mind rich and brilliant thoughts.

3.   Even if you find his/her conveyed ideas irrational or senseless, still learn to respect and appreciate. No idea is ever wrong or right. It only depends on one's perception.

So the next time you exchange a conversation with someone, and your subconscious mind starts rejecting the thought, discipline yourself. Appreciate, value, and respect the idea of your neighbor.

Assess consequences of actions or ideas

There was once a fable of a mountain goat who jumped and fell off a cliff. At the end of the story, the moral lesson was very straightforward. Look before you leap. Yes, it is also a way of developing your critical thinking skills. Always assess the consequences of actions and ideas. You have definitely heard in the media many stories that ended up in tragedy simply accounting to this lesson. In fact, most failures occur because of the failure to assess actions and ideas before they are made. Regret always happens in the end and none of us would want regret in our lives. We are the only ones responsible of our decisions and when taken for granted, these could cause damage to many.

Assess your ideas and actions by:

1. Asking – Ask yourself before spreading ideas you read online. How much damage can unverified information do to others? How will people look at you after sharing a point without proper verification? Even if the extent of the damage is insignificant, you must always avoid spreading ideas without any supporting facts.

2. Considering others' perspectives – Before spewing harsh judgment, think about the person who said the idea first as well as his perspective. Keep in mind that being open-minded is part of a critical thinker's character. You'll shed some light on the working thought construct behind the idea, then you can be more critical about the point after seeing where it came from.

Be willing to consider multiple perspectives

Critical thinking is not one way thinking. It also requires considering other options and multiple perspectives. A genuine excellent thinker has the great capability of coming up with a myriad of options whenever needed. This is also applicable when communicating your thoughts with others.

1. Ask yourself, how would I react if I were in the other person's shoes? Think of his/her point of view.

2. When facing a problem and you come up with a certain solution, again, ask, is this the only solution? Are there other options possible?

Having multiple perspectives means having a multi-lateral mind. Sometimes we might feel contented whenever we are able to come up with a certain solution to resolve a problem, but that shouldn't be the case. Always come up with a number of perspectives. The more, the better.

So the next time you find yourself facing such a challenge and you come up with an answer, stop and list down some more options. This is a great way of training your mind to produce multiple perspectives.

Examine diverse points of view

This skill is closely interrelated to the 15th item which talks about considering multiple perspectives. The process of having a critical, multilateral mind doesn't stop at considering options. You also have to examine those options and points of view. Do these until you come up with the perfect and most appropriate answer. Now this doesn't only apply to self-thinking. Also apply this in comparing others' points of view with your own.

Analyze the points of view by:

1. Examining the differences between the presented idea and your own idea – Your objections on the idea will help you determine the extent of differences between the two points. Take note of these then continue with the next process.

2. Think where the point came from – Ideas came from a person or basing it on another people's perspective. Take note of your differences as well as the person who said the thought. Keep in mind that diverse perspectives are brought by different influences like socioeconomic status and culture. Research about the source and see these differences. At this point, you'll understand more about the other point of view.

After knowing the differences in perspectives, you can use the gathered information the next time you'll study an idea. You'll be able to get others' perspectives faster through practice.

Promote academic conversations

Achieving critical thinking is a far-fetched dream without having prior knowledge. That is why it is highly recommended to promote academic conversations and engage in dialogues that foster critical thinking. Sharing conversations with fellow thinkers flourishes and nourishes one's mind. They will hand you brilliant ideas and thoughts which are suitable and even advantageous for your critical thinking development. That is why it was said earlier that one must analyze and be aware of his/her group influences. Spending time with idealists will help you, but listening to and engaging with irrational thinkers might just as well break you. However, exchanging conversations is not a one way process. Do not let them do all the talking. Share your thoughts and ask questions as well. This is one of the best exercises to foster your critical thinking. Join groups with the same endeavors; listen to keynote motivational speakers and approach successful and reputable people in your community.

Promote intelligent conversations through the following tips:

1. Choose the group and the right time for intelligent conversation. It's true that you should maximize your time for intelligent conversations as much as possible for improving critical thinking. However, there are times when it's impossible to strike up intelligent conversations, especially when it's time to have fun like reunions. This is also the same with time. The best time to have intelligent conversations is during casual dinners, lunch with some colleagues, or some friends who are into the same discussions.

2. Set an idea or issue to discuss. Choose any topic as long as it's not an offensive topic. Settle with science or recent issues where you can exchange facts with others.

3. Listen to other parties' ideas. Remember to listen carefully and understand their perspectives as discussed in "Examine diverse points of view" sections.

4. Present your points according to facts. Remember to present your points in the most logical and factual way possible. Have supporting details to establish your ideas properly.

Intelligent conversations will help enhance your thought process while promoting your goals to others.

Make reasoned decisions

Excellent decision making is a characteristic of critical thinking. Decisions should not only be made promptly, but must also contain acceptable reasons behind them. A good decision is not made in an instant; it must involve supporting details that would qualify it to be reasonable enough. And making decisions is a part of daily life, which is why critical thinking must always come into play. Was there ever a time where you made quick decisions and later on you regretted that certain decision? If only you would have spent some more time in assessing that decision, things would have turned out better. We do not want this to happen again. So the next time you find yourself involved in a critical decision-making situation, take note of three or even five reasons why you should consider the decision. If you find yourself lacking in reasons, then perhaps it's not a good decision after all.

Make logical decisions by performing the following steps:

1. Always look forward to the consequences – Decision-making can be fairly easy until the consequence hits you. Hence, it's best to always look forward to the consequence while you are still at the beginning. Consider if it will affect other people and your life negatively. If not, then go on with your decisions.

2. Always have a backup plan behind your decisions – You may have planned something with reasoning, but something might come up that can affect the outcome. Remember that critical thinking includes looking at the deeper aspect of any idea. Understanding that extraneous variables may affect the decision's outcome will help you be more prepared for the consequences.

Always be well-informed

Searching for reasons, analogies, explanations, and analysis is a difficult job to deal with if you have inadequate information. Having an adequate reservoir of knowledge is one vital tool in critical thinking.

1. Read books and read the good ones, particularly those which are factual and informative.

2. Be updated with local and international current events.

3. Do not ever limit yourself with what you think you already know. Learning is a never ending process from cradle to grave.

4. Even when assessing others' ideas or making decisions, the factors you consider must be based on your knowledge and on collected information.

5. Try to observe successful people and thinkers in your community. Notice that they always spare a part of their time in learning.

6. Keep on learning and take time to go over your learning over and over again. With a well-informed mind, you get a developed mind.

Think critically on a daily basis

Achieving and harnessing critical thinking doesn't happen overnight. An old quotation says, "Rome was not built in a day." The same goes for an excellent mind. Changing your thinking habits every single day is the key here. The time would come where your habits would eventually change for the better. Developing a critical mind has stages.

1. You start by being the unreflective thinker. An unreflective thinker is one who is unaware of significant problems in his/her thinking.

2. The second stage is a challenged thinker i.e. one who is aware of problems in thinking.

3. Then you become a beginning thinker when you try to improve but without regular practice.

4. Next is a practicing thinker who recognizes the necessity of regular practice.

5. Eventually you become an advanced thinker when you advance in accordance with your practice.

6. Our ultimate goal is to become a master thinker. This happens when skilled and insightful thinking becomes second nature to us.

Now determine which stage you belong to and work your way up the ladder using this book.

Follow problem solving steps

Do you still remember what our mathematics teachers have taught us in grade school to follow steps in solving math problems? The same actually applies when solving any type of problem. With these eight vital steps, problem solving would be easy.

1. State the problem as clearly and as precisely as you can. Whenever possible, only take problems one by one.

2. Study the problem and determine what kind of problem you are going to deal with. Set aside the problems which you have no control over. Only concentrate your efforts on those that you can potentially solve.

3. Seek information you need and make sure you collect an ample amount of information.

4. Analyze and interpret the information you have gathered.

5. Figure out your options for action.

6. Evaluate your options. Take into account their advantages and disadvantages.

7. Adopt a strategic approach and use this strategy. For example, you might use direct action or a wait-and-see strategy.

8. Lastly, monitor the implications of your actions. Be prepared to shift your strategy or statement of the problem as more information becomes available.

Don't forget these eight steps so that solving a problem, no matter how big, would be much more comfortable.

Expose yourself to complex and challenging questions

Sometimes, or rather oftentimes, we evade difficult and challenging questions. We do this because of the fear of not answering the questions right. Turning our backs on complex questions is not helpful when we aim to improve our thinking. Whether we get the answers correctly or not, it is a beneficial act for us. Exposing ourselves to complex and challenging questions exercises our mind and critical thinking skills. Being always at ease is dangerous because it disables mental stress, thus hindering mental development. On the other hand, the more you push your mind to the limit, the more that critical thinking improvement is within your reach.

Expose yourself to challenging questions through the following:

1. Watch debates. Intelligent discussions like debates are the best places where you can hear challenging questions. You don't have to attend an actual talk if you are unavailable. Watch them online as documented videos are uploaded online. Some websites dedicated to sharing big ideas also post talk videos.

2. Take note of the questions that appealed to you. Several challenging questions will hit you intellectually. Write them down and use them later for your own training.

3. Listen to how these questions are answered. Watch and listen to how the debaters answer difficult questions. Write down their points and check some notable facts they shared.

4. Assess the answers and questions. Think about the answers critically by asking whether experts have a point or not. Object if you find their points questionable then research for the answers yourself.

5. Participate once discussions are available. Watch out for possible talks in your office or community then make sure you participate. Topics may be different, but you can apply your new skills in answering difficult questions.

Engage in reflective thinking

Reflective thinking is a form of self-assessment. No matter how you consult others to rate you, you would be the one person to exactly know how far you are in improving your critical thinking. Why? Because only you and no one else knows what's going on in your mind. Your thoughts cannot be read by others and the effort you are making to improve your thinking is always unseen. This is where reflective thinking comes in. It is used so that you will be able to grade yourself and assess your improvements or deficiencies.

1. At the end of a long day, find a quiet spot in your room. Make sure there are no distractions. Also make sure that you have done everything you need to do and the next thing after this is just to sleep.

2. Sit down, close your eyes, and meditate.

3. Ask yourself these questions:

    *   Am I committed enough to improve my thinking?
    *   What did I do today to improve my thinking? What did I did not do?
    *   Am I improving my thinking?
    *   On a scale of 1-10, how would I rate my thinking skills?

Do this every single night right before going to bed until you develop an automatic system of reflective thinking.

Think independently

Obviously, thinking must be done independently. It is never wrong to consult others when making decisions or dealing with problems. However, doing this frequently, and leisurely, is detrimental for our minds. Letting others think for us discourages our minds to generate wondrous ideas. Over the long term, it will be a bad habit. It is degenerative. And if you are this type of a person, start thinking on your own.

Except when gathering information, do not ask others until you come up with an idea of your own—an idea produced by your brilliant mind. Only when you come up with one can you only consult others and ask for their respective ideas. Never be tempted in letting others think for you, no matter how difficult the question is, no matter how good that other person is. You are brilliant. You can do it on your own. Think independently.

Train yourself effectively to perform independent thinking with the help of the following points:

1. Always remember that you are a different person. You have your own ideas influenced by your beliefs, upbringing, experiences in life, culture and others. Therefore, your thoughts will be unique from those of others. Your ideas may be the same at some levels, but subtle differences will make you unique. Be committed to your ideas and avoid going with others' if you don't share the same opinions.

2. Avoid feeling guilty. Some people go with others' ideas simply because they feel guilty. This immediately defeats the concept of improving critical thinking. Be assertive to stand firm on your ideas instead of letting guilt get the best of you.

Demand clarification

Always ask for quality and clarification questions. Was there ever a time that you heard of a wondrous idea from a reliable source but didn't understand it? Now that isn't a wondrous idea at all. You only thought it was wondrous because it came from a reliable source. It could be a famous speaker, a well-known preacher, or even a best-selling book.

No matter how credible a source is, when our minds are not able to synthesize a certain idea, then it becomes useless. Nevertheless, the same kind of idea is rendered by irrational people. Always demand for clarification. Do not remain timid wondering about the answer. After all, it was their idea, and they should be responsible in clarifying it.

Several tips on how to ask for clarification:

1. Ask your question effectively. The problem with clarifying a point is that the person asking is not clear with his questions. Ask what's precisely about the idea confuses you so the presenter will be able to discuss it properly.

2. Ask nicely. You're probably confused, but it doesn't give you the right to be rude. Ask nicely and clearly to get your needed clarification.

3. Avoid reacting negatively right away. Don't react immediately to the idea if you're confused. You probably missed some points and this resulted in confusion. Reacting negatively will backfire because you'll come across as not listening to the presented point. Ask, process, and then react.

Give attention to details

To be an excellent critical thinker, focus on details to derive meaning. The key to interpreting complex ideas is to break it into smaller pieces, and you will need to see the smaller pieces of a complex idea to be able to synthesize it. This can be done through focusing on details.

1. For example, when determining the feasibility of a business project, you cannot simply answer yes or no. Look for the details. Is it affordable? Will the project be attainable within the time frame? Do I have enough manpower? Is the planned location appropriate? Is the project profitable?

2. Now to make it simpler for general decision making situations, consider the four W's (Who, what, where, why) and the one H (How). Examples of questions to ask:
    *   Who are the people involved and affected by the decision?
    *   What are the consequences of the decision? What are the factors that may affect the decision?
    *   Where should be the decision or the project take place?
    *   Why is the decision important?
    *   How should the project be carried out?

Remember that these are sample questions. They could be different depending on your project and goals, but they should follow this pattern.

Be innovative

Explore alternatives to seek better and new solutions. You can do this through becoming innovative. Do not be afraid to try. Do not be afraid to take risks. Your mind is a powerful tool that can generate innovation. You must not settle in your comfort zone and be contented with what you already know. Also, do not be contented with what the world and the people around you already know. Read over your history and you will notice that all the great men became who they are because of the innovation they contributed to mankind. These great men are excellent thinkers, and you are about to become one. With adequate knowledge, start exploring alternatives and you will find better or new solutions. Ask yourself always, are there alternatives? Can I generate an alternative? You will be amazed that you can be an inventor in your own way.

Some tips on how to be more innovative:

1. Have the right mindset. Mindset is important in being innovative. Trying out something new means there is the possibility of making mistakes. Keep in mind that there's nothing wrong in making mistakes and it's a part of the learning process in honing critical thinking.

2. Understand that innovation is important for everyone. Use the concept of innovation as a thing for everyone to keep you motivated in experimenting. For example, researchers base their studies on past studies, which is a form of innovation. Their goal in researching is to find something new that will be beneficial for their studies. You should do the same in order to improve.

3. Prepare yourself. Being innovative is easier said than done. You'll find it quite uncomfortable at first since you'll be stepping out of your comfort zone. Prepare yourself for the challenge and keep your eye towards the goal of being a critical thinker.

Have a healthy lifestyle

Now you might wonder why this item appeared in an article about improving your critical thinking. Yes, living a healthy lifestyle is necessary for the mind's improvement. A sound mind must be housed in a sound body. You can never unleash your full potential if your physique is not at its best state of well-being. How can you make the best decisions if you are sick? How can you engage in complex problem-solving if you feel tired? How can you seek and analyze information if you are dull? Now that it all makes sense to you, start to live a healthy lifestyle. The mind is indeed the most powerful organ of the human body. However, it may be corrupted if the systems in the human body don't perform at par with it.

Lifestyle change like the following are basic, but will work wonders for improving brain power:

1. Flush out toxins through diet for faster brain processes.

2. Sleep and naps are vital to refresh your mind.

3. Spend at least 30 minutes of aerobic workout daily to improve oxygen intake and circulation in the brain and the body.

4. Take a full and healthy breakfast daily as your body's fuel.

5. Meditate to reboot brain processes.

Take the road less travelled

In other words, do not follow the crowd. Poor thinkers often feel pressure to do things just because others are doing them. This is the bandwagon mentality, or the "me too" syndrome. This thinking problem is characterized by an instinctive drive to follow the crowd. You are not a poor thinker; you are an excellent critical thinker. You are capable of deciding on your own. You produce options. You innovate using the brilliance of your mind. So whenever you feel the pressure just because others are doing it, pause for a while. Give time to notice and wait until there is evidence to prove that it's the right action before you give in. If you could not come up with a strategy behind following a crowd, sooner or later, you might find yourself trapped in uncomfortable and unsustainable territory.

Tips on how to go against the flow:

1. Be confident in your individuality. Don't think of the norms. Just because the majority of people believe in the same concept doesn't mean that they're right and that you're wrong. Be confident in your thoughts and opinions. Don't be afraid to express them and stand firm on your beliefs.

2. Don't think of yourself as an inferior being. Others may seem more dominant than you, which can make you think that your opinions are insignificant. Rather than feeling inferior, think of yourself as an individual with as much equal right to express your ideas.

3. Go against the flow right from the beginning. Many people think that they'll go with the norm then try breaking free later on. The problem is that they find themselves eventually unable to go against the norm and finally losing their individuality. It's best to get away early on before it's too late.

Be creative

Creativity is one thing common among great thinkers and successful people. In the real world, creativity is not only luxury, but a necessity and a survival skill. A critical thinker is a creative person. We all use our creativity in different ways, but we must follow a common process. Once the process is understood, you can apply it intentionally at any situation needed. It boosts your creativity and efficiency and it also strengthens your initiative.

The process has four stages:
1. Just like when creating a work of art, you need to have that picture in your mind before painting. Explore the issue, find relative data, and figure out the most effective path to resolve it.

2. Come up with the best and new ideas—ideas capable of initiating change.

3. Develop those ideas. Examine them and rebuild them if necessary. Polish your ideas until they shine.

4. Lastly, implement and take inspired action, such as when an artist displays his creative artwork in a gallery.

Be creative. You are an artist. The life you are painting is your masterpiece, and your paintbrush is your mind.

Know when to move on

You might be equipped with so much optimism that you always fight for your idea. But if things aren't working out so well, change your strategy. You did not change your decision to reach your destination; you only took a different route leading to it. This is one characteristic very few have. It is called flexibility. People who have this know when their preferences are getting the best of them and are able to re-strategize and change direction. Do not be obsessed over endless possibilities. If you've done a thorough job and things aren't going so well, move on, and still be on target. Having this skill is like having a good map. Now it's up to you to drive your critical mind to your goals.

Moving on to another route is a challenge, but keep the following tips in mind to help you get past this hurdle:

1. Remember that nothing is wasted. Many individuals are not comfortable moving on because they think the effort exerted on the first route is wasted. However, nothing is wasted in this case. It is part of the learning process. The journey outweighs the result.

2. Take inspiration from other experts. Great minds also experienced the same hurdles in life. They also took different routes and some even waited years before they finally fully developed their critical thinking. They simply kept their eye on the prize. If they can do it, you can do it too as long as you're committed to it.

Have a purpose

When facing decisions, there is always a purpose attached to it, perhaps a goal that you would want to achieve.

1. Always have a purpose and identify it.

2. Once you identify your purpose, include it in every process of your decision making.

3. Make sure your purpose is clear and always articulate it to yourself. A purpose must always be a starting point and never an end point. This is fundamental in developing a critical mind. It is very basic: have a purpose, read it aloud to yourself, and you may even write that purpose down and place it somewhere that you would never fail to see.

Stop before you start

Yes you read it right. Stop before you start. Think before you start. Having self-awareness is a fundamental trait of an excellent critical thinker and all successful people. Having self-awareness means you should determine your limitations and weaknesses as well. Once you know your limits, you will know what aspect to improve upon, you will know where to ask for help, you will know where to bend, and you will know where you'll be doing fine. This skill will help you be clear about direction and limit the unnecessary amount of effort you have to exert along the way. This will save you tons of time ahead. So before you even start with anything, stop and think.

Stopping before starting can be easier with these tips:

1.   Don't let emotion get in the way. Some individuals fail to think before starting because they let their emotions get the best of them. Even if the idea is seriously against your point of view, don't let it get to you and continue listening to the point until you understand it.

2.   Set your filter system. Filter the words you'll use to make sure you won't offend others with your words. Use the right words and rephrase your ideals in the best way possible to avoid coming across as rude.

3.   Stop to set your tone. Tone is everything in introducing your idea or your objections. As long as you have the right tone, your delivery will sound better and thus, you will avoid arguments.

Trust your instinct

They say trust your instincts. Well, sometimes, you do need to pay attention to persistent hunches. There are situations when you feel like you just can't let go of an idea, but it's too tough to make a case for it and make it happen. So what are you going to do when faced with such a situation?

You may want to consider the following strategies to integrate critical thinking with your instincts:

1. Differentiate instincts from fears. Fears usually mask instincts. Many think that the lack of words to present ideas is caused by their instincts keeping them from doing so. But in most cases, this inhibition is triggered by fear. Hence, people must differentiate if it's fear or instinct that's causing the inhibition. Knowing the difference is essentially knowing what you feel about your idea. If you feel that the idea is making you feel constricted or uninspired, then it's probably your instinct warning you. But if your idea is making you feel out there, expanded or highly passionate, then the negative feeling you're feeling is just fear.

2. Meditate. The inhibition brought by fear and instincts can be stressful and may cloud your mind more. Several minutes of meditation each day will help you calm your mind and think better about your ideas.

3. Go for it anyway. Even if it's your instinct warning you, you may still want to go for it anyway since your goal is to be a more innovative thinker. Study your ideas, research, establish your point, add some confidence, and go for it.

Most success stories are of people who took action even if the idea seemed wrong at that time. Trust your instinct yet always analyze it, consider all factors, and visualize outcomes.

Diversify

A critical thinker embraces diversity. One of the most powerful skills of a great thinker is the ability to leverage diversity. We are talking here about diversity of thought or the art and process of leveraging and maximizing different ways of thinking. A critical factor to consider is to always recognize where you are strong and where you are not. If at a certain field you know you are not adept, seek others who are. And exert effort in improving this. Listen to their thoughts and listen to the new directions their thinking can provide. Learn to diversify and be open to others' perspectives.

Diversify with the following tips:

1. Be like a blank sheet of paper. Diversifying includes clearing your personal bias. Think of yourself like a sheet of paper which is clean of contents to allow space for new information.

2. Listen to a lot of ideas. Expose yourself to other ideas by listening, reading, and watching debates and news.

One step at a time

Critical thinking involves processes and stages. Skipping certain parts of these stages is highly dangerous and can even lead to serious problems. Take one step at a time. One example of skipping stages is focusing on the wrong issue. You learned earlier that the first step in a problem solving process is to identify the issue clearly and precisely. Failure to do so will automatically ruin the whole process. Another example is implementing a half-baked solution or one without the appropriate analysis and examination. People often skip stages with the thought that it will save them time, but the fact is, every time you skip stages, the more you lengthen the time of the process. It might even cause you to start all over again. We all have preferences for different parts of the process that may lead us to unconsciously skip essential steps that would have made an innovative idea a reality or would have been the turning point in getting the right solution for our problems.

Taking one small step at a time can be challenging, but these tips will make the process simpler:

1. Be patient with the process. Patience is indeed a virtue in this process. Don't hate yourself or feel down because you're taking it slowly but surely.

2. List down the procedures. Whether you just want to improve critical thinking in general or strategic planning, listing down the steps needed for planning will help you stay more focused.

3. Be your own critic. Critique yourself once you seem to be going off track in planning. Stop yourself if you begin focusing on unnecessary issues to get yourself back to the right thought process.

Have a happy spirit

Be happy, smile, and maintain a sense of humor. Critical thinking is believed to be mentally stressful which is why a lot of people don't engage in practicing it. Actually, it is really mentally stressful. That is why this tip was given for you to be able to cope with the rigors of critical thinking. You can never think straight, after all, if everything seems like a matter of do or die to you. An excellent thinker has the skill to laugh and see the humor in situations. This can help in maintaining clarity of thought and perspective. It also fosters calmness, optimism, and positivity.

Tips to be a happier and effective critical thinker:

1. A good laugh will help. Look for something that make you laugh. As they say, everyone needs a good laugh. Loosen up by watching or reading humorous material then laugh.

2. Integrate humor with critical thinking enhancement. This is more beneficial because it goes with the goal. Do this by watching humorous shows with witty lines and characters. It will help you become wittier while exposing yourself to other ideas.

Have an open mind

It is easy to distinguish a close minded thinker from an open minded one. A close minded thinker is not open to discussions and only firmly believes in his or her own set of beliefs and opinions. This is a very unacceptable attitude for one who wants to develop a critical thinking mind. Improving your thinking involves processing new input. A close minded thinker cannot be convinced or reasoned with. Imagine a glass full of water. It cannot contain new water anymore because it is already full. You must empty it before it can contain new water. Such is the human mind in the learning process. However, having an open mind doesn't mean accepting every point of view. Having an open mind is having the willingness to exchange thoughts in searching for the truth.

Several tips to help you become a more open minded person:

1. Do away with personal biases. Just like in other tips in this book, freeing your mind of personal and belief biases is the first step in being open-minded. You'll be able to accept other people's ideas. Again, you don't have to go with the idea, but you will just listen to the point and use the information for discussion.

2. Look at the other person without bias. Some people fail to be open minded simply because they don't like the other party. This personal bias brought by disliking will make a person too "deaf" to listen to their points.

Examine authority

A critical thinker doesn't automatically accept authority. It is not wrong to admire their looks or antics, but believing them all the time is. It doesn't mean that what you hear from Hollywood stars, politicians, or professional athletes is always right. We do this unconsciously because we were accustomed to the appeal to authority a lot of companies use as an advertising gimmick. We are made to believe that if the personality says that this is great stuff, then it must be. But you are a critical thinker now. You have the right to examine, or even question, whoever that personality might be.

Examine authorities and their ideas easily with these tips:

1. Research authorities' credibility first.

2. Object to the presented ideas instead of believing them immediately.

3. Don't forget that authorities are paid to make a product or idea look good.

4. Examine through additional research to see if they believe what they are saying.

Resist impulsiveness

Impulsive decision making is what we aim to correct in developing our thinking skills. Impulsive decision making often leads to poor and regrettable decisions. When we are under pressure, temptation arises to make an impulsive decision. Some may reason out that it is better to have a wrong decision than to have no decision at all. Well, that is rarely true. Indecision is an indication of thinking problems and poor decision making skills while impulsiveness only accelerates and assures the consequences of poor decisions. So the next time you are under pressure, stop and think to resist impulsiveness.

Make yourself extra resistant to impulsiveness with these tips:

1.   Always remember that being impulsive usually has a negative outcome.

2.   If you've been impulsive before and ended up with a negative outcome, remind yourself of the lesson you learned at that time.

3.   Breathe, relax, and meditate if you're feeling the pressure to make hasty decisions. This will give your mind space to think.

Be realistic

Critical thinking can be most effective if it is based on reality. Your thinking can be more productive if you are able to perceive, interpret, and analyze reality. Reality is objective. It exists independently. Its presence is not parallel with your wishes, goals, ambitions, and desires. A critical thinker must be objective. Being objective is distinguishing "what is" from what you might want to believe, or perhaps separating "what is" from what is more comforting to believe. You should thus value objective reality.

Tips to help you be more realistic in your thoughts:

1. Read, read, read the news to get the facts.

2. Make sure that you're reading factual information backed by proper research.

3. Always look at others' perspectives to push away some preconceived realities that don't apply to everyone.

Eliminate ambiguity

An excellent critical thinker always exercises the power of thought to establish clarity. Ambiguity is a symptom of irrational, incomplete, and sloppy thinking. Now once you experience this state, examine your principles, your knowledge, your promises, and the efficacy of your thinking process. Knowledge is the only weapon you can use to retrieve clarity from confusion and uncertainty.

Do away with ambiguous thoughts with these additional tips:

1. Know the right words that describe your thoughts clearly.

2. Always base your ideas on facts.

3. Practice to deliver your thoughts clearly even if you're with people who understand you best.

Be consistent

Improving your critical thinking is a routine to consistently seek problems in your thinking. Being consistent is a good sign of careful and thorough thinking. A critical thinker always applies consistency and logic in whatever that needs to be considered. Inconsistency is just used to obscure the truth. So if you really want to improve, be consistent.

Attaining consistency is easy as long as you remember these tips:

1. Don't leave space for complacency. Practice makes perfect and you should practice consistency at all times.

2. Look at your ideas from a different perspective.

3. Ask insights from another person and tell them to give their ideas without being biased as a result of friendship or relationship.

Practice empathy

A critical thinker always withholds judgment until he or she is sure that he or she has adequate information. This is called empathy. You should not judge others until you fully understand the whole situation. By practicing empathy, you minimize the risk of making impulsive decisions and half-baked conclusions. On the other hand, once you have adequate information and you have examined it well, do not hesitate to make decisions. Understand others to develop a deeper insight. With a deeper insight come wiser decisions.

Be a more empathic person with the following tips:

1. Look at ideas from another person's perspective.

2. Practicing kindness in looking at another person will give way to empathy.

3. Leave behind personal bias against the person and focus on ideas and insights instead.

Know your learning style

For learning to be most effective and conducive, know your learning style. This is the learning technique wherein you absorb knowledge the fastest. For example, if you prefer hands-on experience, then engage in it. If you prefer lectures, readings, and discussions, take part in these. If you prefer group experiences, then go out and find a group.

Take advantage of the following tips to discover your learning style:

1. More than preference, take note of the learning materials that work for you. Know which materials deliver the ideas to you well.

2. Aside from materials, look for a mentor whose ideas and style appeal to you. Emulate their style without losing your individuality.

3. Know the best time where you find studies more effective. Whether you're a day or a night person, study at the time that works for you so as to maintain your focus.

Eliminate negative talk

Negative thinking is a self-talk-sub vocal conversation by reinforcing critical judgments and attitudes about you. You convey negative images over and over again. Here are examples of this kind of thinking: I cannot do anything right, I must not trust anyone, I'm not as smart as everyone else, I am ugly, I am not loved, and school is a waste of time. When taken for granted, this kind of thinking will influence your decision making in an undesirable manner. This is a serious thinking problem and thus must be replaced by more positive self-talk and self-esteem. Counseling is a good solution to eliminate this kind of problem.

Apart from the aforementioned ideas, take note of these tips:

1. Look for affirmative statements online to counteract the negative talk.

2. Look at yourself as a strong and confident individual.

3. Think of the people who believe in you and let their support deal with your negative self-talk.

Have the passion to learn

Anything you want to achieve can be easily attained with the burning desire, commitment, and dedication. Passion is the fuel to keep us doing what we must do. With enough passion, you will love your work wholeheartedly since your mind and heart are set to winning your goal. Learning is the key in improving critical thinking. Be passionate in learning.

Find and keep the passion through these suggestions:

1. Give yourself time to rest to keep you from being burned out.

2. Think of professionals and big minds in the field. They are already household names in their own right, but they never stop learning.

3. Always remember that you're probably good, but there's always space for learning and improvement.

Improve listening skills

Listening is a very vital skill that we often take for granted. When engaging in conversations, what you hear is what you get. You may have probably been in a situation when in the middle of a conversation, you realize that a person asked you a question that you didn't even hear. Or perhaps you daydream during a classroom discussion. It happens to us all; it indicates our deficiency in this skill. The better you listen, the more information you will obtain. With more information come better decisions.

Improve your listening skills through the following:

1. Go back to the basics of taking listening comprehension quizzes online.

2. Being open-minded is the key to having better listening skills.

3. Know the difference between listening and hearing. Keep in mind that listening is a skill while hearing is merely the ability to identify sounds.

Always maintain perspective

Maintaining a sense of perspective amidst an important matter is a characteristic of a critical thinker. Do not balance in any situation and always view the matter on a larger scale. Ask yourself this question; is it really as critical as it is at the moment?

Make sure to maintain perspective through these ideas:

1. Accept the fact that change is the only permanent thing in this world. The importance of an idea or situation will change depending on time and other variables.

2. Aside from importance, check if some plans or ideas are necessary. Discard unnecessary thoughts because they will only become distractions.

Learn and apply

The only way to improve critical thinking is to learn and apply. Commit yourself to continuous learning and go over related references. Of course, apply these methods in your everyday life until it becomes natural to you. These 50 ways to improve your critical thinking are proven methods to improve your mind power. The work is up to you to put these into action and do your assignments. Go over these notes once in a while, and never miss out an item.

Conclusion

As a conclusion, I would like to congratulate you! I commend your effort and willingness to improve your critical thinking. Keep in mind that these strategies must be applied in your daily life. Test these ideas, integrate them into your routine, and build upon them every single day. Soon you will notice that these ideas play a vital role in shaping your life. You have interwoven 50 strategies and constantly look for opportunities to apply each one of them. Your practice will bring advancement until insightful and skilled thinking becomes natural to you. Improve your thinking and improve your life!

ABOUT THE AUTHOR

Christ Lewis is the author of Non-Fiction, Self-Help books. He loves reading books about personal improvement and any self-help books. He always tries to level up himself and improve himself to be better in any things all the time.

He has his own business and he's also a writer. His inspiration is to write what he has learnt or experienced in the past. He would love to continue his intention to spread his knowledge to his family, friends, goodreads friends, and other readers all around the world.